Trespassers

poems by

Christopher Locke

Finishing Line Press
Georgetown, Kentucky

Trespassers

Copyright © 2016 by Christopher Locke
ISBN 978-1-63534-067-9 First Edition
All rights reserved under International and Pan-American Copyright Conventions.
No part of this book may be reproduced in any manner whatsoever without written permission from the publisher, except in the case of brief quotations embodied in critical articles and reviews.

ACKNOWLEDGMENTS

I would like to thank the editors of the following magazines where these poems first appeared:

Agenda, (London); *Audubon*; *Bare Hands Poetry*, (Ireland); *Blueline*; *Gargoyle*; *The Literary Bohemian*; *The Meadow*; *Moon City Review*; *Mudlark*; *The Nervous Breakdown*; *Northern Cardinal Review*; *Nowhere*; *Shake The Tree*; *Terrain*; *Upstreet*; *War, Literature & The Arts*

Publisher: Leah Maines

Editor: Christen Kincaid

Cover Art: Christopher Locke

Author Photo: Sophie Locke

Cover Design: Elizabeth Maines

Printed in the USA on acid-free paper.
Order online: www.finishinglinepress.com
　　　　　also available on amazon.com

Author inquiries and mail orders:
Finishing Line Press
P. O. Box 1626
Georgetown, Kentucky 40324
U. S. A.

Table of Contents

I. THERE

Ordinary Gods 1
Day of the Dead 2
How to Write a Poem and Save Yourself from Drowning 4
Daily Commute 5
For You, Good Price 7
No Siesta 8
Running in Mexico 9
EcoTours, Ltd 10
Aubade 11

II. HERE

Porcupine 15
February in Salt Minor 16
Happy 17
On Learning We Would Not Lose the House 18
Late Return 19
Visitation 20
Lake George 21
What The Dead Know 23
Trespassers 24
The Last of the Open-Heart Astronomers 25

For my students: always the better teachers

I. THERE

Ordinary Gods

Not ashen with the rage of *Popocatepetl*
smothering blue nimbus of Mexican
sky, one body after another flung deep
into its untoothed char, Aztec sacrifices
even Cortés couldn't stomach, his breastplate
mutely glinting to Franciscans everywhere,
which was nowhere. Not the volcano's
sulfurous hands raising its body of smoke
higher than the wound itself; 17,000 feet
above the nonbelievers who thought steel
and gunpowder could quell superstitions. No,
not them. Or others with names like hornets
nesting between the intake of breaths:

Cihuateteo, Itztli, Tezcatlipoca: Gods of stone,
the nocturnal sky and ancestral memory;
god protecting the spirits of women
who died in childbirth. Not even these.

I am talking the *God of Purified Water:*
the man slung miraculously with three
plastic jugs across his shoulders shouting
away the gray sheets of dawn as he climbs
the hills of my neighborhood; or *the God
Singing His Ice For Sale,* raising heads still
drool-warm from their pillows; the *God Running
the Scales of His Pan Flute,* music announcing
he is here to sharpen your knives, standing
loose-limbed in the alley, a mere few pesos,
cutlery flashing like the bright destruction
wrought by Cortés those years ago, when gods
were still plural and damnation not yet known.

Day of the Dead

I pull my drunk friend out from inside
a bush, and think he must be looking
for the Mexico he's read about: a story
of The Beats, myth of newsprint photo
with ringleader Ginsberg looking insane,
neck roped in marigolds as he smiles
next to a burro, Kerouac to his
right and already sideways off clay
tumblers of shadow-cool mescal,
the pink bake of sun unseen above
them in San Miguel de Allende.
What else explains my friend's
impersonation of Neal Cassady,
himself found dead not far from
here after a marathon of cards
and booze, the cold iron of westerly
tracks his final bed, dumb enough
to pass out and freeze to death high
up in the desert night. Dumb. So I
yank him hard off the cobblestone,
stand him up in this city echoing
with wedding cake churches and wide,
empty plazas, and slap his face hard.
"Wake up," I tell him, and hail a green
and white taxi trundling by, throw him
in the back and hand the driver 50 pesos,
an address. "*Gracias por todo*," I say, and
shut the door, thinking, one less gringo
to fill a jail cell tonight. I stand next
to a park fountain gurgling blood
red in reverence to *Dia de los
Muertos*; three tiny skulls made
of sugar sit on the ledge, forgotten,
or left in tribute. Tomorrow, my friend,

shy and hungover, will call with some
version of sorry, and I will say no
problem, though it is, and turn back
to an altar made of dried corn and
flower petals, a small, clear glass
of rum left for a friend recently
dead, another drinker, because
tradition dictates you leave loved
ones something they treasured in this
life, regardless. But I am no hero. And
now, sitting on the edge of the fountain,
I see the same stars we all see, high
and tangled in their indifference, steely
grains fastened to a sky that once held Dean
Moriarty outside Denver; lights Kerouac
believed strong enough to serve as halos.

How to Write a Poem and Save Yourself from Drowning

Don't start with the dubious hieroglyphs
of someone else's dream. You need grounding.
Substance. Like my daughter throwing up,
her coughs and tight chokes a rusted screw
turning wet until the flakes give way, the sigh
of worry both my wife and I register, the second
time in one week she's been sick here in Mexico,
bacteria pounding her blood with its gray fists
and bilious demand. Yesterday, brass trumpets
popped the air in glinted voice as a funeral
procession marched slowly past our house,
the men in jeans and cowboy hats, the women
in great plods of garment flung bright around
their bodies. The back of a Chevy pick-up
foamed white with carnations and lilies
curling like an ocean's memory of happiness
as the pageant snaked onward. Yet the drivers
behind in gridlock were patient, unflinching:
silver crucifixes swinging from rearview mirrors
like stars ancient to things I will not understand.

Daily Commute

But before I could remember the name
of these angled white birds, the way
they filled the skies above our rented
house in Mexico, I had to first anoint
a camel spider in great chuffs of poisonous
oils, unfair really, being trapped as he
was in the *terraza* corner writhing like
the possessed I remember from my child-
hood church, when I believed men could
call God down from the rafters. And there
were also the dogs to deal with at night,
their barbed cries stringing the air
like broken Christmas lights, tuneless
and savage, unnerving in their confident,
dreamless yaps, envious of their brother
coyote running free in the desert, chained
only to his boundlessness, leaping brush
and cacti and the tiny scorpions which glow
under a black light like absinthe, creatures
we fear the most when strolling our garden's
dahlia or slipping on our unchecked shoes.
But the birds, stork-like and mute, moving
above in clumps like highway traffic: first
four, then three, then the lone flyer I feel
the most for as he has no one to share his day.
They are dependable every 12 hours, a clock
punching numbness glued to their expressions,
if that's what birds have, expressions.
The common sparrows will go rustling
in the nearby bamboo, gossiping the green
leaves past frenzy, but these white ones,

their wispy legs dragging useless behind
them, glide silently above us, joyless
and sober, forcing our daughters to point
while splashing in the pool, marvel these
bright tufts made brighter by the desert's
retreating light, all going home, all done
for the day. Yes, that's right: *Snowy Egret*.

For You, Good Price
—Chiapas, Mexico 2012

The agrarian shock of plow
and tree; miscellaneous scrub
of horse pinned to the horizon.
And the corn stands exhausted
in wilted silence, as if great

crowds of it herded into place
before police declared the gathering
illegal. Yellow flowers rise like
different-sized arms straining:
Pick me, pick me, I am strong

enough to work. Shattered cinder
blocks lay heaped in derision,
their dust beaten out of them
like hope, like the wrong answers
to a hammer's only question.

The sunlight drops to its knees
behind the palmetto as tiny birds
buckshot the air. Later, above
the sleeping city, the stars wait
their turn to dream our faces silver

as a girl sews a toy bandolier on her
Commander Marcos doll, placing
him in a pile with others that will
fetch a sum tourists from the north
will believe is an absolute steal.

No Siesta
—San Miguel de Allende

The color of heart sliced
to its blue, the sky
frames adobe mansions
too expensive to house
taste. Broken bottles embed
the tops of their high walls
like a glassblower's dream
of revenge. The bronchial
mesh of mesquite trees stiffens
the air, and birdsong unplugs
its numerous fountains under
this blue of tight hours, of heat
translucent in its heavy broth
of light. Until at last, up the
cobbled street, a lone girl pulls
a small red horse on tin wheels
so as to make the shadows
ring with her love.

Running in Mexico

My wife double knots her laces
then stands, hopeful she'll be un-
daunted by the thin Jaliscan light
and broken beer bottles glinting
near our doorstep like a drunkard's
shattered necklace. She bounds one
cobblestoned street after another,
running with a cold bottle of Gatorade
in her pack, a small knife she carries
in case of dogs, or worse. The lake
she circles shoulders a rowboat, but
no one is rowing, the water fetid
and jade-like, making the shimmer
almost beautiful. Tight bunches of hollow
wrappers scuttle her feet—one empty
of its chili lime peanuts, another its chili
lime potato chips; flavors, we've realized,
they can't get enough of here. Last
night, the fruit-seller, a girl no older
than one of our daughters, told us
the mango wasn't ripe, but no matter,
just skin it, sprinkle it with lime and chili,
and *presto*, you've got yourself a meal.
The mango looked bigger than a human
heart, and as I held it in my hand I
wondered how many beats my wife's
would need to keep carbon dioxide
from plundering her cells, to fill her
lungs the way grocery bags fill the trees
as she navigates these roads, running,
avoiding the catcalls tossed her way
from cantina doorways, her feet pounding
dust back into the cracks and edges;
the places where sunlight comes to die.

Ecotours, Ltd.
—Ixil Triangle, Guatemala

Olive-shined and crumpled,
eucalyptus leaves huddle weakly
atop steaming rocks, unmarrow
your sinuses with a darker fragrance
shocking you back to life. You

breathe the stinging deeper, gaze
a few chicken feathers mixed in,
and smile: you've another hour
in this dripping cave, and then it's
a hot air balloon champagne dinner
high above the Mayan landscape.

The brochures were right: you *couldn't*
ask for a better deal, the tour sold
cheap and easy as the human bones

just a dig of earth away, 30 years
since a bulldozer shamed them
into ground, muddied tree roots
curling about skulls popped open
by gunfire bright enough to translate
terror into cornstalks shattered red.

But that was a long time ago.

And you've artisanal rum
to sample, hand-sewn tapestries
to consider, and these cute little
jade earrings that your girlfriend
would just die for.

Aubade

It was the last good thing we heard: a bus
station bird more dismal than some errant
mudsplash split between the arches. But
its voice bathed the concrete in light, sang
our attention back into something brighter
than our tiny struggles: the bag handle catching
in a harried taxi; the luggage wheel stuttering
its last complaint until snapping like a tooth.

Once again, we had asked for nothing and nothing
was bartered for in favor. It is what we'd grown
accustomed to in Mexico, but still managed
to surprise us when most needed. The bus had
just arrived amongst the fumes, saddening us,
proof that this was all ending, and our crowded
bags were hauled into the vehicle's dark maw;
six yellow tickets handed back in a tidy exchange.

Our adopted city curved behind us, its hills pressing
the air like clavicles unskinned, our home now
abandoned, but more likely indifferent: Guanajuato
at ease with so many streaming faces, so many
hands reaching with plucked desire, the streets
stacked with buildings dumfounded by colors
for which even priests couldn't atone. *But the bird.*

We needed that. Yes. All four of our heads
turned upwards, listening to his watered
symphony as reminder that beauty rises
from the common, caught fluttering
in the breath of every day.

II. HERE

Porcupine

                        We trained
the headlights against its prehistoric,
nubbled shape and waited for it to cross
the road, rain a misery of *forgive me* down
our windshield, me still unsure who needed
absolution: us or some recent past.

                      Almost there,
lumbering yet cautious, blue recycling
bin tipped empty on its side, wind
ringing the chokeberry in the adjacent
yard of a neighbor we haven't met,
three weeks since moving here to Maine;
long parchments of seaweed line our shore
like maps discerning where we've been,
where we hope never to return.

                     The porcupine
finally passed, and when my daughter
wondered out loud if something helped
guide it, I imagined a mouse as crossing
guard, small sign gripped in his hand,
one of those bright orange vests made
by someone who loves him, who needs
the world to see him clearly in this rain.

February in Salt Minor

The snowplows bring their gray news
just like the ocean waves outside our window,
morning walks always a puzzle of refuse
flung from the Atlantic's bayed vaults:

lobster traps sullen in their green crush
of wire voiceless against the shore; painted
buoys stiff on the sand like rockets out
of breath. We fill our pockets with beach

stones and let our thighs grow numb
with such frigid persistence, a coldness
rehearsed like our own: the burn of it,
the way ice leaches until all we've left

is stark enough to light a thousand arctic
suns, white and heavy as blindness.

Happy

> But there are no happy endings, because if things are happy, they have not ended.
> —Donald Hall

Portland museum, slight chips of snow
ghosting the windows like ash off
cigarettes; a Maine sky imprisoned
with all the tough angels. We sit in
the building's belly, a café seizured

in beautiful pastries, croissants glazed
like tearful cheeks; popcorn labeled
as non-GMO and therefore, somehow,
healthy. We eat in silence, and I'm thinking
about the Pissarro on the third floor, and

that strange video tower being the only
piece which read "Please Touch", itchy
guards swimming the rooms with hope
you'd drag a finger down a Wyeth
so as to give them a reason. The girls

pipe up, start comparing the best key
lime pies they've ever had, the best
scones: "Nothing spongy," Grace says.
Sophie nods in agreement, mouth full.
My wife offers "What if we opened

a restaurant and called the kid's meal
a 'Happier Meal,'" and it's my first
genuine laugh of the day. "That's
great," I say. "What would we serve?"
My wife shrugs, noncommittal.

And the nicest exchange we've
shared in days ends as quickly as
as it started, so we turn back
to our daughters, their talk silly,
natural, and yes, almost happy.

On Learning We Would Not Lose the House

The news dismantled sorrow; saved
us. Like the condemned sung free,
we rejoiced until raw and shouting,
danced the green from the lawn's
thick pelt. We were so loud we could
not hear the future, could not see
November or those deputies apologizing
from a doorway no longer ours, gray
ropes of sunshine wrung useless between
the trees. For now, we only knew
this moment. Someone fired up the grill
as the children formed hunting parties,
entering the woods in a giggling line.
A bottle was passed from one adult
to another and dragonflies buttered
the air; one even traced my daughter's
shoulder before attaching to the back
of her head. And as I reached out to
touch it, I noticed it glowed smoky
pink, barely a cinder—not enough
heat to light even the fires of the poor.

Late Return

Harmless really, the dog arthritic
    as icy rust, uncoiling fragile barks
at Sophie running out to see me before
    I drove off. I was trapped in my car,
the dog owner between us all sunflower
    and grandmotherly charm. So I
motioned, had to say *Please, your dog, my daughter...*
    And then the part I didn't want
to admit: *She was bitten before.*
This new dog made Sophie freeze
tight as December maple, juiceless
    and heavy, and the owner smiled, telling
her, "It's okay, I have seven grand kids
    of my own," and took the dog away.
Yet in the car, unable to leave, shaking,
    repeating to Sophie I'm sorry, holding
her, I remembered the first time all those
    years ago: the way the dog disheveled
her, splashed her into the grass, tried to unSophie
    her, teeth locking in place like gears
oiled to their own need, and me too late
    to stop it; that stone I still carry.

Visitation
    —for Sophie, age 8

        Not the boot-sucking clam bed,
Sophie stuck up to her knees, tide out and rocks
gulping at their own nakedness.
                Not the trails scraped in snowmelt
winding the nearby woods where she lost
her blue mitten as we spied deer prints
and dog prints thinned to crystal relics.
                Not the quick
slip to pavement, leg rubied in bright
scratches, lower lip quivering, incapable
of holding so many indignities in such short
order. No. It was Sophie uttering her desire,
limping now, to just once see an owl's face
"…in real life," until all of us stopped dumb
in our tracks on that wet country road
as one appeared, barred and mute
in the twilit branches above. We stared
a good, long time until I hooted, and the owl
lifted away into its deeper silence.
                And there was Sophie,
shy again, walking upright, even as we returned
to the house where all the windows were dark.

Lake George

Jefferson proclaimed it the most
beautiful water, and high up on
this ridge, the aster and goldenrod
touching hands, we can see why:
it stretches blue over thirty miles,
islands like well-groomed heads
rising luxurious and clean. Sunlight
ghosts between the milkweed as my
daughters complain they're thirsty,
ironic as most all we see is water.
Earlier, in the rock and roll sushi joint,
Gracie nibbled rice as if in a contest
to underwhelm, and I worried her
teenage years before me, asked if she
ever felt that food was an obstacle,
something she could prove wrong.
She shrugged her shoulders and sipped
green tea, and I understood we were
moving apart; two trains blameless
toward their own horizons. It saddens
me, and as we make our way to the bottom
of the hill, Sophie discovers a pond burping
with frogs. She laughs and swoops
them up, collects them into a found
bucket until Gracie shoos them out,
tells them to run away. And as I
try to intervene, console one and
admonish the other, I think I'm
no different, trying to set free every
mistake that still holds me weightless,

circles my life like ashes around the moon.
But as my daughters fall into argument,
small shouts of accusation, I stand useless
between them, hands apart, fearing this
is the moment the two always knew
was coming, the day I must choose.

What the Dead Know
> *There are not enough pleasures*
> *to simplify the spirit.*
> —Charlie Smith

The dead do not visit me at night; at 3 a.m., I do
not sense their vaporous bodies gliding over my
bed to reveal some mortal prophecy: "Avoid
the morning train," or "A fire awaits you at the bakery."
Nothing. Just me split and pulled from the char

of a receding dream, alone in my sheets as night
counts the insomniac stars, the neighborhood
crushed in heaps of silence as no dog unravels
on its chain, no loitering Camaro sprays *Van Halen*
against our petrified rosebushes. How can the dead

know I would prefer their blank company, their insolent
calm to all this ordinary nothing clogging the avenues
of my sleep as I lie here and think of my stepfather
and how almost every night he sees whole lines
of the dead enter his room as if taking numbers, closing

in on him, telling him they await not in fire but in silence,
and he will be addition by subtraction, and that they
will lift him up to the others breathing behind the clouds
in their melancholy and their robes, lift him by the wrists
as if he were just cut down from some holy machine.

Trespassers

The snow, bread-torn and
scattered, patchworks this field
and this wood, this narrow chasm
cum walking path through which
the three of us falter. My wife
walks ahead as if in a different
movie, a silent picture that ends
with her arrival somewhere else,
radiant and alone, and its all I
can do not to wish her luck. Sophie
doesn't notice, or is kind enough
to pretend otherwise, and instead yanks
an adolescent maple down by its neck,
bounces its snowy crown to dust,
laughing. Her joy lengthens the distance
between us, compounds Gracie's absence;
it's been months since she joined these
hikes—*what did she call them?*—to nowhere.
Now she spends weekends with friends, my
fear she's repeating what I did at her
age: raiding liquor cabinets or agreeing
to the next great high, images of her
discovering new, beautiful countries
of loneliness. I chase Sophie uphill
then down, ice-weary and heaving,
dodging tiny snowballs made by tinier
hands. My wife leans against a spruce,
"Pull her close," she commands, so I do.
She snaps a photo with her phone, stores it
in a place I no longer have access, a border
I am no longer allowed to cross.

The Last of the Open-Heart Astronomers

Mowing a dark sea
of lawn behind your home,
you sweat and shove the engine
like a raw-mouthed god, push it
churning above a great furnace
of yellow jackets until they are so
enraptured, so possessed, they burst
skyward and fan a tornado of cursing
debris. So you turn from your
machine, the grass, the cloud
of pain engulfing you with its
miniature complaints, and run
blind towards some other country,
one that only speaks in low, soft
tones, and you can't believe,
as your knees decide to pray,
that you've become this helpless,
this incapable, until they descend
on you like evening, and tired of
naming stars, you close your eyes.

Christopher Locke was born and raised in New Hampshire. He received his M.F.A. from Goddard College and has published four previous chapbooks of poems and two full length collections: *End of American Magic* (Salmon—2010) and *Waiting for Grace & Other Poems* (Turning Point—2013). The recipient of two Dorothy Sargent Rosenberg Poetry Fellowships, Locke has received grants in poetry from the New Hampshire Council on the Arts, the Massachusetts Cultural Council, and Fundacion Valparaiso (Spain). He currently serves as the nonfiction editor at *Slice* magazine in Brooklyn.

www.ingramcontent.com/pod-product-compliance
Lightning Source LLC
LaVergne TN
LVHW041514070426
835507LV00012B/1565